MOMENTUM
LETTING LOVE LEAD

OTHER BOOKS BY JOHN-ROGER

Awakening Into Light

Blessings of Light

Buddha Consciousness

Divine Essence

Dream Voyages

Dynamics of the Lower Self

Forgiveness:
The Key to the Kingdom

God Is Your Partner

Inner Worlds of Meditation

Loving Each Day

Loving Each Day
for Moms & Dads

Loving Each Day for Peacemakers

Manual on Using the Light

Passage Into Spirit

Psychic Protection

Q & A Journal from the Heart

Relationships:
Love, Marriage and Spirit

Sex, Spirit & You

Spiritual High

Spiritual Warrior:
The Art of Spiritual Living

The Consciousness of Soul

The Journey of a Soul

The Path to Mastership

The Power Within You

The Signs of the Times

The Sound Current

The Spiritual Family

The Spiritual Promise

The Tao of Spirit

The Way Out Book

Walking with the Lord

Wealth & Higher Consciousness

For further information, please contact:

Mandeville Press, P.O. Box 513935, Los Angeles, CA 90051-1935
323-737-4055

jrbooks@mandevillepress.org
www.mandevillepress.org

MOMENTUM
LETTING LOVE LEAD

SIMPLE
PRACTICES
for
SPIRITUAL
LIVING

JOHN-ROGER
with PAUL KAYE

Mandeville Press
Los Angeles, California

Mandeville Press
P.O. Box 513935
Los Angeles, CA 90051-1935
323-737-4055
jrbooks@mandevillepress.org
www.mandevillepress.org

Printed in the United States of America
ISBN 1-893020-18-5

There is the Game of Life and the Game of Love.

Most people are playing the Game of Life,
trying to make life work.

Life already works.

How we bring loving into it is the big key.

That's playing the Game of Love,
and it's by far the bigger game.

—John-Roger

I *would not waste my life in friction
when it could be turned into momentum.*

—Frances Willard (1839-1898)
Educator

Love is the strangest thing that I know,

You keep it around by letting it go,

And you follow close and you follow slow,

And love will take you where love wants to go.

—Unfinished Love Song
from "Songs for the Loving Heart"

CONTENTS

Acknowledgements

We would like to thank the following people for their invaluable contribution to bringing this book into print.

Jan Shepherd for her loving "noodges" and unflagging encouragement. Joan Oliver for shaping and crafting the book and keeping her cool even in the midst of our many idiosyncrasies. Shanti Einolander for her seamless editing. Marie Leighton and Angel Gibson on the Mandeville Press team for their gentle guidance and caring. Stephen Keel for his wit and expert touches. Betsy Alexander for her wisdom and experience. Shelley Noble for her creative flair in designing both the cover and interior of the book. Stede Barber for her design and production expertise. Vincent Dupont for his infinite patience in navigating this book from its inception to completion.

FOREWORD

The essential message of this pithy and profound book is that the supreme activity of this world is to love and then to love some more. The authors, John-Roger and Paul Kaye, present us with the lineaments of love as seen in a dialogue between Love's essence and Love's existence. Bold, evocative, even mantic statements are met with reflections for practical applications. Together, these serve to startle and provoke our own inner dialogue. Suddenly, we become philosophers and psychologists of love. We discover that since love is the essential core of our human nature, indeed the cosmic code that renders the unfolding of all life and time, we know more than we thought, we remember what we had forgotten. Love, as Dante said, moves the sun and all the stars. To this we would add, it was love that flung us forward from its initial paroxysm in that microsecond of time that exploded into the evolving universe, seeking partners and lovers in creation. Reality grew through its lovings and affinities, atoms to atoms, molecules to molecules, bodies to bodies, groups to groups, world as lover, world as self. The God in all things is finding expression in the affections that make the pattern of all connections. As humans, we are godseeds planted in the field of time and space, and nurtured and grown through our loving relations.

This book is a celebration of the truth that a new natural philosophy based on love as the creative force of evolution is emerging everywhere, and this lure of becoming finds renewed expression in the rising archetype of the Beloved of the Soul. Quite simply, we are attempting to figure out how to work together as partners, not only in our relationships and jobs and communities but with the planet and the cosmos at large. And, in so doing, we must recognize that in each other, there is the divine being for whom we have searched. The loving energy that drives our lives, drives the life of the entire planet. Like cells of a single body, we are inextricably intertwined. We are the Earth, extended in self-conscious reverence.

Teilhard de Chardin once wrote, "The day will come when, after harnessing space, the winds, the tides, and gravitation, we shall harness for God the energies of love. And on that day, for the second time in the history of the world, we shall have discovered fire."

What can this mean for the evolution of our present troubled world? It suggests the evolutionary energies of love—the capacities inherent in love that could, if harnessed, open up vistas of transformation, culture, human development, and world development virtually unknown today. What does the harnessing of the energies of love mean to the evolution of the Soul, the healing between nations, the growth in intelligence and design, the sacralization of science, and the humanization of our social forms, resulting in a true coming together of peoples and nations?

As we love more, we see and accept more: we honor each other's pain, beauty, struggle, and path. With love we become more intelligent and creative, for we are open to the patterns of intelligence from the whole network of life. We come to glimpse the wonder of life in its infinite forms, and the wonder that is within us. Quite simply, with love we are able to exceed our local conditions. We evolve.

John-Roger and Paul Kaye have given us here the most valuable of gifts. They have shown us how to live each moment as an occasion for loving, and, in so doing, have offered us the keys to the Kingdom.

Dr. Jean Houston
Ashland, Oregon

INTRODUCTION

People often say that love will cure the world.
But this is not exactly true.
It is loving that cures the world.

Loving is action. Loving is manifestation.
Loving is movement.

Loving is the consciousness of giving.

This book is about being loving in the moment.

For years I have wanted to know: Is there a simple solution to our problems, our issues, our challenges in life? After much searching, I have concluded that no matter what we face, we can handle it by being in the moment. "In the moment" is where we can find all our answers. The trick is to bring ourselves into the moment.

What's more, there is another dimension to being in the moment—and that is to be loving. This is the loving that springs from the depth of our being, our spiritual heart. So, the key to life is to be loving in the moment. Being loving in the moment is an option that is continually available—a choice that everyone has the power to make. It takes enormous strength to stay loving in the face of inner and outer challenges, and the distractions of daily life. But it's a choice that is well worth making.

Being loving in the moment is practical spirituality. Practical spirituality is about applying spiritual concepts to day-to-day living. You don't have to try to be spiritual. You already are. But you may have to undo the effects of conditioning to discover your fundamental nature, which is love.

I invite you to use this book to discover ways to engage in the bigger game, the Game of Love. The chapters include simple Practices that provide ways to begin putting into use the ideas presented. Between chapters are sections called **Reflections on Loving** that are designed to assist you in attuning to love. These sections, which focus on such themes as *relationships, challenges* and *self-mastery*, can also be used as a spiritual practice. Re-reading and reflecting on the text is a simple way of bringing your awareness to loving in the moment. The quotes in the book, unless indicated otherwise, are by John-Roger.

The ideas in this book are not specific to any religion. They are based on universal principles found in the world's wisdom traditions. There's no need to adopt any particular beliefs, or give up your existing faith or spiritual practices, to find these tools and techniques useful.

Ultimately, spirituality isn't learned from just reading a book. Question the ideas presented in these pages, try out the practices, allow these principles to come alive inside you. Spirituality must be grasped intuitively and experienced directly by each one of us. The voice of your loving becomes clearer as you practice listening to it. The spiritual heart always knows the truth.

CHAPTER 1

THE WISDOM IN IMBALANCE

It's a good idea to involve yourself in discovering who you truly are. That way, you can change the things that are not working for you and create positive movement inside of you.

Who wouldn't want a perfectly balanced life: great relationships, good health, plenty of money, and an exciting career—all at the same time? If you can do it, terrific. For most of us, it seems that there's always *something* out of balance. Something lacking, in other words.

Perhaps you meet an attractive person and fall in love, but your new lover has expensive tastes you can't afford to satisfy. Maybe you have good health and a great job that pays well, but you've been unable to find that special person to share your dreams. Possibly you have a great relationship, but you're depressed because your job is unfulfilling. You may even have a great relationship, a great job, and lots of money—but your health isn't very good, so you lack the energy to enjoy your good fortune.

For some people, pursuit of a balanced life is all-consuming. You can hear the tension in their voices as they talk about trying to find equilibrium. The unspoken message is: "If everything went my way, if I could just control it all, *then* I would have balance—and life would be great."

Unfortunately, life doesn't work that way. We've all heard the saying, "The only constant is change." Everything in the universe is

It is important to keep moving and not let yourself get stuck and stagnant in any aspect of your life.

Keep moving in the direction of your loving.

in a state of flux. If you took a sample of your blood and looked at it under a microscope, you'd see a lot of movement. Moment to moment, everywhere in the body, some cells are dying off, while others are reproducing. Even the book you are holding in your hand only gives the illusion of permanence; it's a hive of activity at the subatomic level.

The four areas of life we commonly deal with—relationships, health, finances, and career—are in constant motion. On rare occasions they may seem to be in balance. But what most people don't realize is that the very act of trying to keep your life in perfect balance actually destabilizes it. As soon as a system achieves equilibrium, something shifts.

On a spiritual level, of course, the situation is different. However unbalanced things may appear to be from our limited human perspective, in a spiritual sense everything is always in balance. What makes that a problem for us is that, often, we don't like the way things are.

But there is wisdom in imbalance. Imbalance creates movement—and movement gives rise to a dynamic, engaging life that is full of learning, creativity, and growth. Once your life is in motion, there's a natural force that keeps it moving. That force is called *momentum.*

Take a moment to find out where there is imbalance, or movement, in your life. **Practice 1: Where's the Momentum?** (below), will show you where you are now, so you can track the changes as you work with the ideas in this book. You will notice that I refer to this exercise—and the others in the book—as "practices." I use this word because it suggests what you need to do to make spiritual principles work—*practice* until they are a regular part of your life.

PRACTICE 1

Where's the Momentum?

Virtually all of life's activities fall into four areas: relationships, health, finances, and career. These are the areas where we experience most of our problems and challenges. Take a few moments to look at your life to see where there is the most movement right now. The area of greatest movement might be the one in which you have the biggest problem or issue to resolve. Or it might be the one you would most like to improve overall.

Often, we can experience movement as discomfort or dissatisfaction, but it's important to remember that where there's movement, there's also the greatest opportunity for change.

In the space below, rate the four areas of your life on a scale of 0 to 10, with 0 indicating *no satisfaction or fulfillment*, and 10 indicating *complete satisfaction or fulfillment*.

Relationships: _____
(This area includes all your important relationships: spouse, parents, children, friends, co-workers, God, etc.)

Health: _____

Finances: _____

Career: _____

Identifying an imbalance in your life doesn't mean you have to rush out and try to bring it into balance. Rather than resisting the imbalance, or taking a position that lack of balance is bad, you can just relax and accept it as what is happening in this moment.

Despite what your conditioning may tell you, there is seldom anything wrong in most situations in your life. We often label experiences "wrong" when they're not going the way we want them to, or the way someone in authority has told us they should be going. Once you make that distinction and start to see imbalance as movement rather than as deficiency, life becomes an adventure. Instead of continually trying to "fix" situations, you'll start observing your experience to see what you can learn from it.

————————————————

GETTING YOUR LIFE GOING

Everybody in your life can assist you in awakening your loving.

Everyone can help you get in touch with the many aspects of yourself that are within you.

Many of the difficulties we have in life occur because we stopped moving. If we stop moving physically, there is a build-up of waste in our cells, which may lead to toxicity. If we stop moving emotionally, bottling up negative feelings instead of allowing them to move through us, the result is tension and contraction. If we stop moving mentally, we can become fixed and closed-minded, instead of open and receptive.

One way to set your life in motion—to create the momentum for change—is to ask yourself what inner quality you would like to have more of in your life: Peace of mind? Love? Happiness? Make it a quality that, if you had it, it would enable you to feel content and fulfilled, regardless of the circumstances in your life.

"Regardless of the circumstances" is the key here. Let's say that the quality you want more of is happiness. If, for you, happiness depends on meeting the right person, or having the right job, or earning enough money, then your happiness is conditional.

As you continually involve yourself in your own inner movement of awareness, your awakening will happen in its own natural rhythm.

That's *impractical* spirituality—living from the outside in. *Practical* spirituality is just the opposite—living from the inside out. True happiness isn't conditional; it doesn't depend on circumstances being just right.

The quality you choose should reflect the essence of who you are and what you value, so that no matter what happens in your life, the quality will remain a constant. You will know in your heart that your life is worthwhile, regardless of how it looks to the outside world. The quality you choose should be relevant to where you are in your life right now, not just where you hope to be in the future.

Sometimes it is easier to identify the quality you value most when you see it in someone else—someone you admire or someone who has inspired you. It could be a relative, perhaps, or a teacher or coach, or a historical figure or spiritual leader.

What quality comes to mind? _____

Imagine the impact on your life if that quality were fully awake and alive within you right now.

REFLECTIONS ON LOVING

Love is difficult to define.
We might say that love is the essence
that brings forces together and holds them
in a "position" relative to one another.

When we look at things simply,
we can say that our cells are "in love"
with one another, because they stand together.
If they weren't, they would separate from one another.

The experience of love cannot come from a book
or be contained in words. It can only be experienced.
Many people use the words of the Bible or
other sacred texts as a weapon against others,
and they destroy just as effectively as if they were
using knives or swords or guns.
In loving, no one has to defend anything or attack anything.
No one has to win; no one has to lose.
In loving, if you lose,
the winner will help you pick up the pieces.

23- Let Love lead ex.
53- Clear Neg Energy

Love is given to everyone, just as the sun shines on everyone. Not everyone, however, wants to stand in the sun. So, you are the one who determines the level of your experience with love. Love sits by you until that time when you will let love flow through.

Letting love flow through is very easy.
All you do is move to a neutral position—not one of belief or disbelief, not one of judgment or prejudice, but one of receptiveness.
As soon as you judge, you strike against love.

Take the attitude that no matter where you look, no matter what you see, it is a manifestation of love.
That which you see is love in front of you.

Love may be many different sizes, shapes, and forms, but it is all love.

CHAPTER 2

LETTING LOVE LEAD

If you enter your inner world in love,
and you maintain that love,
you can live more freely and effortlessly.

Most of us are trying to make life work. But the truth is, life already works. Life is doing fine. It was here before we came, and it'll be here when we're gone. The Game of Life just keeps rolling on. The issue isn't the Game of Life, it's the Game of Love. What we really want to do is bring more loving into our lives.

Note that I said more *loving*, not love. There's nothing wrong with love. Love is the essence, the core, the harmony within us, the prime mover of our lives. But loving is love in action. Love comes alive when it is shared with others. The more it is shared, the more dynamic it becomes.

Loving is constantly in motion—experiencing, expressing, giving. The loving nature doesn't just say, "I am love," while doing nothing. Being loving is the greatest gift you can give yourself and others. There is nothing in your life—or anyone else's—that loving cannot heal.

Loving is an inner momentum towards health, wealth, and happiness. This kind of loving isn't emotional love. It's not about possessing or controlling anyone or anybody. What we're talking about is spiritual loving. Spiritual loving is neutral. It's not

Love awakens us. When you experience the spiritual heart— your loving nature— unlocking and unfolding, thank God from your deepest being that this is happening to you.

indifferent or uncaring; it's impartial and unconditional. Nothing is excluded from unconditional loving.

You could say this book is a course in loving. A master's course. To become masters of loving, we have to go through an education process. This is not like going back to high school or college, however. There are no textbooks or term papers or exams, no foreign languages to learn, nothing to memorize. Everything you need to know about loving is already inside you. All anyone else can do is guide you in discovering your own loving nature.

Most of us have no idea that we can be masters of loving. We race around looking for someone or something to fulfill us, not realizing that what we are searching for has been available to us all along. Our biggest task as human beings is to learn to be loving. As we move in that direction, every area of life begins to open up.

LOVING IS THE KEY

Throughout this book, there are simple techniques and practical approaches that can support you in *letting love lead*. When I talk about letting love lead, I'm referring to a very profound inner movement that comes from the depth of our being. Putting love in charge is not how we normally live; usually, we let our reactions and ego lead us. Though love is all around us, we seldom give it our full attention; there are so many other places where we focus our energy.

It's amazing how easy it is to give up our loving nature. We're conditioned to deriving our worth from outside ourselves—from what other people think of us, from what we achieve materially, from what we look like. "I don't really know who I am," we may say to ourselves, "but if these people love me, I must be okay."

That's another example of living life from the outside in. It's an empty promise, because if, in the next moment, people stop loving you, or don't look at you the way you want them to, you will no longer feel okay. When others withdraw their love, you find yourself withdrawing, too, and contracting. Contraction is a kind of pulling back—physically, emotionally, or mentally—that closes us down to life. The objective of this book is to move you to a state of expansion, of opening to life and fully embracing it.

The loving heart shoots up like a fountain, into all of life. Whoever encounters a loving nature is lifted. As you express your loving, everyone around you is touched and awakened. When you reach into the unconditional energy of Spirit, you don't experience love; you are love.

✦ When you are in contraction, you can begin to move into a state of expansion by coming back to the question, *"Where does love lead me right now?"* Love always leads you into living from the inside out. It allows you to stay within yourself and realize that:

(*Who you are is enough.*)

Regardless of what anybody else thinks, you can love yourself.

You can love your mistakes as much as you love your successes.

As you hold on to these truths, you will start attracting people to you who will support your inner process. Try it and see. Make a commitment that, just for today, you'll let love lead. (For suggestions on how to do this, see **Practice 2: Letting Love Lead,** below.) Whenever your mind tries to distract you with negative thoughts, or self-doubt, or comparisons with other people, just tell it: "I know you're there. You're always there. You're not going to go away. But today I'm not going to let you bother me, because I want to experience something else."

PRACTICE 2

Letting Love Lead

Much of the time, we go through life letting our reactions and our ego run the show. How would our lives be different if we followed love's lead? Try this exercise and find out:

- *If you're tense, or in a rush, or bothered by something, stop and ask yourself: "What would happen if I let love lead in this moment?"*

- *Then, listen inwardly for guidance. You may receive it through an inner voice, an image, a thought that pops into your mind, a "gut feeling."*

- *Check out any guidance you receive. If it could bring harm to you or others, don't act on it. But if it points you towards health, wealth, and happiness, towards fulfillment and expansion, you can then move in that direction with confidence.*

This technique can work in any area of your life. Think of an area you wish to improve. Sit in a comfortable, safe place. Allow your attention to drift inward. Ask yourself, *"If I let love lead me in this situation, where would I go and what would I do next?"*

In the midst of a challenging situation, it takes great strength to even ask yourself the simple question,

Do you love someone, or are you "in love" with them? There is a difference because if you are in love with them, you can also be out of love with them.

If you love them for what they do, then you may not love them if they don't do what you want or expect of them. But if you love who they are, it doesn't matter what they do, for you love them beyond their behavior.

"How can I let love lead me now?"

If at first the answers don't come easily, don't be discouraged. Just getting to the point where you can ask the question shows that your intention is good and that you're moving in the right direction. With practice, before long you'll come to see this as one of your most powerful tools for listening to your deeper wisdom.

The truth is, we have a choice. Living from the inside out, we become aware of other dimensions within us, and begin to understand that outer circumstances have nothing to do with our ability to love. When we let love lead, we follow the goodness inside us. Then, we have no need to declare anything that happens in our lives as "wrong" or "bad." There's a simple phrase—"I love this"—that can help us remember to look at life from this perspective (see **Practice 3: "I Love This"** on the next page).

PRACTICE 3

"I Love This"

Often, the simplest tools work the best. "I Love This" is one of the most effective practices for coming to a neutral, uplifting place where you can let love lead. Here's how it works:

Whatever is going on in your life—whatever events are occurring, whatever thoughts or emotions you are *experiencing*—whether you like what's happening or not, accept it as *what is* and say: "I love this." (You can add other words, but the essence remains the same: *"I love myself for doing this." "I love myself for thinking this."* Or, if you find yourself in a difficult bind, *"I love this situation."*)

If you find yourself responding to someone in an emotionally reactive way, you can say to yourself, *"I love myself for the way I responded emotionally."* If someone upsets you, you can say, *"I love the way that person upset me."* If you're stuck in traffic, you can say, *"I love being stuck in traffic,"* or *"I love this difficult situation,"* or simply *"I love this."*

What's surprising about this method is that it works even if you don't feel any love when you say it. All you need to do is repeat the words consciously—in other words, pay attention and be fully present when you say the phrase.

Try this practice for yourself. Make a statement of love whenever you can, whatever situation you're in. Observe whether anything changes inside you. Look on this practice as a fun, exploratory adventure.

Of course, if you don't like that idea, you can just say, *"I love this."*

There's a wonderful story, "Augustus," by the Nobel Prize-winning author Herman Hesse, that illustrates the importance of being loving.

It's about a young widow who gives birth to a boy she names Augustus. A magical old man becomes his godfather and grants Elizabeth one wish for the boy. After much hesitation she makes the wish that everyone will love Augustus.

Augustus grows up and despite his bad behavior, everyone loves him. Although he gains fame and riches, he is bored. The more he indulges and the more people love him, the emptier and greedier he becomes until eventually he no longer has any joy and becomes depressed.

Augustus falls ill and decides to end his life by poisoning himself. However, just before he is about to drink his deadly potion, his godfather miraculously shows up and tells Augustus about the wish granted to his mother long ago, which had become a curse. He offers his godson another wish, and, after much thought, Augustus tearfully asks to be able to love others.

The spiritual heart always knows the truth. Whenever you wonder how the spiritual heart can lead you, start by asking yourself, "Is this the right action for me?"

No sooner is his wish granted than his friends abandon him, and he is jailed for his past misdeeds. By the time he is released, Augustus is old and sick. He decides to spend his last years wandering the earth, sharing his love and offering service. Wherever he goes, he cheerfully gives away what little he has—often just a smile and a look of understanding.

One day, Augustus finds himself in front of his old godfather's house. His godfather welcomes him in and comments on how wonderful Augustus looks, and how kind and gentle his eyes are. As they sit together quietly, Augustus dies happy and peaceful.

How often we think that if only everyone loved us, our problems would be solved and we would be happy. The story of Augustus shows otherwise. The message is simple—the greatest reward is to be loving.

REFLECTIONS ON LOVING

Living love doesn't care whether a person is black
or white, male or female, drunk or sober, this or that.
Living love is an expression of the spiritual heart,
which knows no limitations, conditions, or restrictions.

When you look at someone you love very much,
you can feel this beautiful, clear, flowing love.
When you know a love will endure no matter what
happens in this physical world, that love is pure.
When you see parents with very young children or babies,
you often see them sharing the purity of love.
Their love is so uncomplicated, so undemanding, so pure.
That purity is the essence of love.
Take that essence and give it to everyone and everything.
Hold back nothing.
Giving love enhances your love.

When you do not love, you do not fully live.
If you do not fully live, God cannot pour the fullness
of His energies through you into the world.
Those of you who know of the love within and are so filled
with it can give of this love so that others may awaken to it.
In this way, humankind might become
more tender and loving.

You do not have to love personalities.
People are not their personalities.
You are not your personality.
You know that you are not your mind; it changes too often.
Your emotions go up and down.
Your body gets old too fast and develops
all sorts of aches and pains.

Then what are you?
You are living love. You always have been.
Let your loving lead you into awakening and
the discovery of what you already are.

CHAPTER 3

MYSTERIES OF THE KNOWN

You may not always be clear in your direction,
but if you keep moving and let love lead,
the direction will clarify itself.

Many people talk about the mysteries of the unknown. I find it far more fascinating to explore the mysteries of the known. As humans, we invariably know what to do to make our lives better, yet we don't do it. Now, that is a big mystery!

Recall the area of your life—relationships, health, finances, or career—where there's the most movement (see **Practice 1: Where's the Momentum?**, page 7). Now, ask yourself what you know to do in that area that you are not doing at the moment.

It's important to realize that we are talking about what you *know to do*. Not what you *think* you should do, not what you *feel* you should do, not what you *believe* you should do, not what your religion or family has *conditioned* you to do, but what you *know* to do.

Something has probably already come to mind. Say, for example, health is your main concern: You *know* that eliminating sweets will help you lose weight. Or, if finances are an issue, you *know* that putting away your credit cards and using cash will keep you from incurring new debt. Imagine what would happen if you took just one action that you know to do. Perhaps the mere

The voice of your loving becomes clearer as you practice listening to it. You learn to screen out the voices that are not loving. That way, you build a conscious connection to your loving guidance. Then you can be confident love is leading you.

thought brings up anxiety or resistance. That reaction is one of the mysteries of the known.

Once we decide to ignore our own inner counsel, we often go on to pay therapists and counselors and advisers to tell us what we already know (but have ignored). And then we ignore *their* advice as well. Your whole life would change if you had the inner strength to take your own counsel in the first place.

Again, go back to the area of your life you identified as having the most movement. Now ask yourself: *What are you* doing *in that area that you know* not *to do?* Continuing with the health example, maybe you keep a dish of candy around for visitors—but you're the one who eats it.

It's surprising how much you really know. It's not that you always have the answer, but you know the next step to take *towards* the answer. You may not be able to diagnose your own health problems, but you do know when you need to consult an expert who can. **Practice 4: Listen to Yourself,** coming up next, suggests ways to work with your own inner guidance.

PRACTICE 4

Listen to Yourself

We discover what we already know to do by listening within. Often the answer comes in a flash of intuition. Just because we got an answer doesn't guarantee it's a valid one, however. Sometimes what we think is intuition or spiritual guidance is coming from our thoughts and emotions—our wishes and desires—rather than from love.

To find out if I'm listening to the voice of love, I ask myself two questions:

- *Does the guidance I'm receiving promote or enhance at least one of the following qualities: health, wealth, happiness, loving, caring, or sharing?*

- *Does the guidance serve or assist others in some way?*

If the answer to both questions is yes, then I am comfortable acting on my intuition.

If you can't love somebody, it's best to say, "I don't know who they are." That's a clear, precise, and honest statement, because if you don't love someone, you really don't know who they are.

The person you criticize, the one you put down, is not known to you. Anyone who is truly known to you is loved.

FROM A DISTANCE

Often when we don't do what we know to do, it's because we're too close to the problem to see it clearly. We need to take a few steps back—or up. The phrases I use to remind myself of this are, "Get some distance on the situation," and "Get some altitude."

Astronauts who have gone into orbit report having had a transformational experience when they looked back at Earth. Gazing at our beautiful planet, with its aquamarine seas and with white clouds floating around it, they saw perfect harmony.

Imagine for a moment that it's ten or twenty or thirty years ago, and one of those astronauts is circling the planet in his spacecraft, awed by the beauty and harmony he's seeing. He focuses his telescope on your country, then zooms in on your city, your street, and finally, your house. There you are, alone in your bedroom, bawling your eyes out over an immense tragedy—your girlfriend (or boyfriend) turned down your invitation to the prom. Which view of the world is "correct" in that moment: the perfect order and harmony the astronaut is seeing—or the chaos and tragedy in your life?

Neither view is right or wrong in itself. Which one is "correct" is a matter of perspective; it depends on where you are. So it goes with most things in life.

If we can get enough distance on a situation, we can usually come to "okay." A little bit of altitude, and we can come to love.

MULTIDIMENSIONAL BEING

Every day, experience shows us that we are not just bodies walking through the world. We are multidimensional beings— brilliant aggregates of mind, body, spirit, imagination, and emotion, all continually interacting. Furthermore, *your* multidimensional being is continually interacting with all the other multidimensional beings around you. Sometimes we don't even realize how much we influence one another on a subtle, energetic level.

Have you ever gone shopping in a supermarket or a large department store and come away feeling exhausted? There are a lot of negative thoughts and feelings floating around unseen in the environment, and, like magnets, we attract other people's negativity. That, in turn, can affect our own energy and mood.

It is easy to pick up on someone else's feelings. Let's say I am chatting with somebody who is upset. Even if the other person doesn't outwardly show that something is amiss, I will be aware of it at an unconscious level, and I'm likely to come away from the

Everything is now.

This is the moment of God's eternity, right now.

Eternity goes into the past and into the future; but it's all now.

There is no place you can think or be that you are not within eternity.

The loving eternity is expressing itself this very second.

encounter feeling uncomfortable. I might assume that the source of my discomfort is within *me*, when, in fact, it might have nothing to do with me. I am simply receiving someone else's negative energy.

This is *not* to say that if I pick up someone's upset, I will also start thinking their thoughts. Rather, what generally happens is that their upset enters my energetic field and impacts on me through my own personal reference points. In other words, I will start thinking about the upsets in my life, not in theirs. I may start mentally arguing with people, or getting angry about situations towards which I normally feel neutral. I may even become mindlessly reactive. What's happening is that the anger of the other person is now playing itself out in my world. Their anger is disguised as mine.

Energetic exchanges like this are going on constantly. The key to handling them appropriately is to *know yourself.* Know your personal triggers—the situations or thoughts that tend to set off an emotional response in you. Then you'll be better able to discern whether the source of an emotional upset is within or outside of you. If you're sitting in a restaurant enjoying a lovely dinner and, out of the blue, you suddenly start getting upset, there's a good chance you are picking up the negativity of someone else in the room.

There's an easy and effective technique for removing others' negativity from your system. It's called **Clear, Disengage, and Disconnect**.

PRACTICE 5

Clear, Disengage, and Disconnect

Let's say you've been with a friend who is sick and you've come away with a heavy heart, or you've gone into a rough neighborhood, or you've been on a crowded train at rush hour. Any of these situations can leave you feeling drained or anxious or out of sorts.

To clear the negativity from your energy field, simply take your hand, place it over your forehead, and silently say, "Clear, disengage, and disconnect through the Light, for the highest good." These words declare your intention to separate from the negativity and come back into the comfort of your own energy field. To learn more about working with the Light, see Chapter 7: **Let Go and Let God**, page 115.

Be *true to your inner guidance, which is your loving speaking to you and leading you. But never follow blindly the guidance you receive. Check it out. That way you learn to trust yourself.*

As you get to know yourself better, you'll become increasingly adept at discerning what's your stuff and what's someone else's. But there's another level on which subtle energy affects you—the energy exchange within your own body.

As research in mind-body medicine demonstrates, when you get sick, the cause is often not strictly physical. If you come down with a cold, for example, an emotional upset you had a week or ten days earlier may have been a contributing factor; emotions can suppress the immune response, leaving the body unable to fight off a virus. Whenever you aren't feeling well, it's worth taking time out for self-reflection. Ask yourself: *What have I been thinking about? Who have I been around? Have I been upset about something? What's going on in my emotional life?* The illness may be directing you to areas of your life where there are issues you need to clear up.

At the same time, you can go overboard trying to analyze the reasons you don't feel well. Sometimes the explanation is simple: you've been ignoring the basics of good health, such as eating right, getting enough rest, and drinking plenty of water. With our hectic, over-scheduled lives, it's easy to neglect ourselves physically and emotionally. In our computer-oriented culture, many of us are moving our bodies less. We're sitting at our desks all day and not getting enough exercise.

Even more serious than lack of exercise is lack of sleep. Sleep deprivation is widespread in the United States. The latest National Sleep Foundation poll found that more than a quarter of the population has sleep problems serious enough to affect their mood, performance, and overall health. Whether by choice or necessity, we're reducing sleep time to a minimum. At the height of the dot-com boom, people liked to boast that they were working "24/7." To me, that was a forewarning of the coming bust. A 24/7 lifestyle is unsustainable.

Don't give for the reward of giving. Give because it is love's nature to give. Do the right thing just because it is the right thing to do. There need be no motive except the love of doing.

Most people will acknowledge that getting too little sleep reduces their efficiency and increases the chances of accidents. But the long-term consequences of not getting enough sleep are even graver. An article in *The Chicago Tribune* summed up the findings of recent research:

"Cutting back on sleep to make more time for work and play might not be as harmless as once thought and could be as dangerous to health as a bad diet. Scientists are finding that [sleeping less], which most Americans do, plays havoc with important hormones, possibly harming brain cells, depleting the immune defense system, and promoting the growth of fat instead of muscle. There is even concern that sleep deprivation may accelerate the aging process."[1]

We can ignore our bodies, but they won't ignore us. There's a joke I like that makes that clear:

A woman in her late 40's has a heart attack, and while she's lying in the hospital she has a near-death experience. She meets God and asks Him, "How much longer do I have to live?" God tells her, "Forty-two years, seven months, three weeks, and two days."

She wakes up and thinks, "Well, if I'm going to live that long, I might as well look as good as I can." So while she's in the hospital, she has a face lift, a nose job, an eyelid tuck, a neck lift, breast augmentation, a tummy tuck, and liposuction in her thighs. After the swelling goes down, she looks fantastic. She leaves the hospital, and as she's crossing the street, Whap! A car hits her, and she dies instantly.

She meets God again, and this time, she's furious. "You told me I was going to live another forty years! What happened?" she demands. "Oops," God says. "I didn't recognize you."

DON'T HURT YOURSELF, DON'T HURT OTHERS

Another thing we know not to do is harm ourselves or others. Yet we spend a lot of time beating ourselves up about one thing or another. "Don't hurt yourself, don't hurt others" is one of the most important phrases you'll learn in this book. It is a universal spiritual principle that has an enormous practical effect.

Here's a situation that anyone who drives will find familiar. Say someone cuts in front of you. There's a tendency to react and get upset at the other driver, particularly if you're in a hurry. But that person doesn't know who you are, and probably doesn't care.

If you ever have the opportunity to help someone, do it. Those acts of loving kindness come back to you when you need them.

Loving is contagious. What a great day it will be when there is an epidemic!

Meanwhile, what has your reaction done to *you*? Your body has responded to your anger and upset as if you were under siege. Your fight-or-flight mechanism has been activated, pouring adrenaline and other stress hormones into your system. Since you're sitting in your car, those chemicals designed to help you fight off an adversary or run from danger have nowhere to go. They're building up in your system, causing a toxic reaction.

It really doesn't help anything or anyone for you to harm yourself in this way. There are other choices.

> You get love by giving, by being of service. If you say, "What do I get back in return?" then you are once again in your own way.

Similarly, not hurting others is the more loving choice to make whenever the opportunity presents itself. Sometimes, even when you are loving, the other person feels hurt or offended anyway. (If that happens, give them a copy of this book! —and remind yourself that you cannot control other people's reactions.) But we can choose not to *intentionally* hurt others. If you still need reasons to follow the principle "Don't hurt yourself, don't hurt others," here are two: you'll be happier if you act that way, and you'll be of service to others simply by your loving presence.

As you stop doing things to hurt yourself, you naturally start to take better care of yourself. And as you take better care of yourself, you start to feel more expansive and reach out to others.

At some point, you may begin to see that life is not a win-or-lose situation. It's a *learning* situation. Whenever something or someone upsets you, you can always find a way to use it for your education, upliftment, and growth.

FROM TENSION TO MOMENTUM

We are here on Earth to learn how to play the Game of Loving. But often, we may find ourselves playing in a field of frustrations, obstacles, and tension. We've all got our "favorites." Maybe standing in an endlessly long line, or being stuck in traffic, or encountering an unsympathetic authority figure is the sort of thing you find most frustrating.

In my case it may be when my flight arrives late, and I'm hurrying to get to an important appointment, but I'm stuck waiting for my luggage at the airport baggage claim. Sound familiar?

Recall that there is wisdom in imbalance. Imbalance creates movement. If life presents what appears to be an impasse, it may just be a perfect opportunity to ask, "How can I let love

Living love is the service of the moment. It is not fearful. It can reach out and touch and share without abusing or corrupting. It brings a blessing simply by its presence.

lead now, in this moment?" When outer circumstances seem fixed or set, the greater opportunity for movement is inner—in the wide range of ways we can choose to respond in a situation. It may take some cajoling, but we *can* shift our efforts from attempting to control outer circumstances and, instead, towards greater cooperation, openness, and awareness. The Game of Loving is never entirely beyond our reach.

I know consciously that getting tense about anything doesn't change the situation, however I find that the less conscious parts of me need educating. Those parts of me seem to open and cooperate when I use humor and loving. Here's a playful inner dialogue I practice with myself in situations when I'm getting a little frustrated or agitated; I exaggerate the relative benefits of getting tense, as opposed to relaxing, in response to the situation at hand.

It goes something like this:

> *By getting tense, I will be able to control the situation more effectively.*
>
> *Now, if I get really tense, then I will be able to control the situation even more effectively.*
>
> *Sure, I can relax, but if I do that things will surely go out of control and then people will judge me for not making an effort.*
>
> *However, if I am tense and I get upset, people will know that I have made my best effort and will not judge me.*

Having reached this conclusion, it is easy for me to see how ridiculous it is to be tense about the situation I am in. By continuing to exaggerate the rationale underlying my initial response, I can see the humor and absurdity in getting upset, and it is then an easy and natural step for me to cooperatively choose relaxation. If I can relax, even a little, I gain a measure of dominion over my outer circumstances, and can begin to move the momentum of tension into relaxation.

You can have a lot of fun doing this kind of inner dialogue when you find yourself in an upsetting situation. The humor and playfulness is in *challenging* your conventional reaction.

With awareness and practice, we can begin to recognize the momentum in difficult circumstances, and use the opportunity to discover new things about ourselves in an expansive way. We're all too familiar with reacting in situations like these, with frustration and tension. We don't have to live that way. *We can let love lead.*

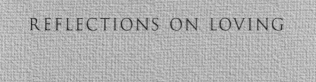

REFLECTIONS ON LOVING

When love comes to you,
don't refuse it by thinking you are not worthy.
You are worthy, or love couldn't come your way.

People often say that love will cure the world.
But this is not exactly true. It is loving that cures the world.
Loving is action. Loving is manifestation. Loving is movement.
Loving is the consciousness of giving.

There is a "taker" part in everyone that says,
"But when do I get mine?" That's the ego speaking.
The purest love is always unconditional. There are no strings,
no conditions, and no expectations of any return.
The giving is pure. If you give 100 percent and love totally,
you need no return. If you love 100 percent,
you can bring healing to anything.

When you come from the heart,
from the center of love,
you do not come from the mind or emotions.
You do not come from the ego,
attempting to control others or
force anything down their throats.

Give love. Give silently. Don't tell people what to do.
Instead, just support them with your love.
That's the best gift of all.

If you want pure love,
then go to where pure love resides.
Pure love is the Soul.
It is inside of you and needs no interpretation.

CHAPTER 4

BEING PRESENT

Now is the only moment.
This is it.
This is all there is.
Enjoy it.
You can still have aspirations and plans and visions;
just place them where you can realistically handle them,
and that starts with right here and now.

Nearly all the ancient spiritual teachings say, in one way or another: *Be present. Be here now. Live in the moment; this moment is all there is.* The question is: How do we do it?

Becoming aware of your breath is one of the simplest ways to come into the present. No matter what is going on in your life, you can always take a moment to focus on your breathing. When you find yourself in a tense situation, for example, you may notice that you are holding your breath. Putting your attention on your breathing can help you relax and immediately be in the here and now. This practice, found in many spiritual traditions, is often referred to as mindfulness, being present, or living in the now.

You may ask, since we're breathing all the time, why do we need to *practice* it? What we're practicing is conscious *awareness* of the breath. Then breathing becomes a concentration exercise that not only focuses the mind but brings many healing benefits as well.

The physiological benefits of proper breathing are only just beginning to be documented. But practitioners of mind-body medicine have long used breathing techniques to treat everyone from advanced cancer patients to trauma sufferers to children with

If you maintain a loving neutrality towards your ups and downs, one day you will wake up and find yourself living in the loving heart, and you will know that all your experiences were but rungs on the ladder that led you there.

Attention Deficit Disorder. An article in the *Los Angeles Times* on stress and breathing quoted James S. Gordon, M.D., clinical professor of psychiatry and family medicine at Georgetown University School of Medicine and director of the Center for Mind-Body Medicine in Washington, D.C.:

> *Slow, deep breathing is probably the single best anti-stress medicine we have. When you bring the air down into the lower portion of the lungs, where oxygen exchange is most efficient, everything changes. Heart rate slows, blood pressure decreases, muscles relax, anxiety eases, and the mind calms.*
>
> *. . . Look around your office, and you'll see so little movement in people's bellies that it's a wonder they're actually alive. Then watch a baby breathe, and you'll see the belly go up and down, deep and slow.*[2]

In the same article Andrew Weil, M.D., clinical professor of internal medicine at the University of Arizona's Health Sciences Center and founder and director of its Program in Integrative Medicine, went so far as to say, "The simplest and most powerful technique for protecting your health is breathing."

The best news of all is that breathing requires no special equipment, no expense, and no expertise. All it requires is your attention. (See **Practice 6: Breathing,** below.)

PRACTICE 6

Breathing

When you find yourself getting tense or stressed, take a moment to focus on your breath. Sit quietly, let your body relax, take a slow, deep breath, and feel the air gently filling your lower belly. Don't force it. Breathe naturally, without straining or pushing. Follow your breath as it moves in and out.

After a few moments, you may begin to feel yourself "being breathed." You're making no effort. The breath is just being received, then let go of. When your mind wanders, as it inevitably will, gently bring it back to the breath. The practice of breathing can bring more joy, peace, and calm to your life in an effortless way. Perhaps, too, it will increase your awareness of the connection between breath and Spirit. When we become consciously aware of that connection, something expansive takes place within us. Focusing on the breath is an accessible and ever-present doorway to our loving.

Try to make a habit of taking short breathing breaks during the day. I recommend three breaks a day, of at least ten seconds each. If necessary, set the alarm on your computer or watch to remind you.

This simple practice can make all the difference in developing a healthier mental and emotional outlook. Try doing it with a group of friends or colleagues, and after only a minute or two you will likely feel the atmosphere of the room change.

Breathing practice—alone or with others—is an immediately available and effective way to focus your attention, open to your loving, and create positive change within and around you.

Being here and now, you can release the tension from your stomach, let the mind relax, and allow the emotions to balance. You may find that you start liking the person next to you. You begin loving everyone.

CHANTING

Another very effective means to focus the mind and open to your loving is chanting. Since the beginning of time, religious and spiritual groups have made a practice of intoning sacred words, sounds, prayers, and songs. Chanting builds up a powerful field of spiritual energy that can change your consciousness. The key is your intention—bringing an attitude of reverence and love to whatever you are chanting.

Mantras are specific sounds or syllables that invoke a spiritual essence. It is said that as you chant, you bring that essence, or vibration, into your own being. I recommend the HU chant. HU is a name of God found in Pali and Sanskrit, ancient sacred languages of southern Asia. Chanting HU silently or aloud, alone or in a group, helps create attunement and brings you into spiritual alignment. As with other practices in this book, you don't have to hold any specific beliefs to do it. Try it, and see if it works for you.

PRACTICE 7

Chanting HU

HU (pronounced like the man's name, HUGH) is a sacred tone. It is one of the many names for God chanted in many spiritual traditions. This simple chant can quickly bring you into spiritual alignment and give you a sense of peace.

Before you begin, sit quietly for a moment and allow your body to relax. Call in the Light to fill, surround, and protect you for the highest good (see **Asking for the Light**, page 125).

Now begin the HU sound. Take a deep breath and as you exhale, chant HUUUUUUUUUU on one continuous note, until all the breath is expelled. Repeat 5 to 10 times, chanting HU each time you exhale.

Then relax for a moment, bringing your attention to the middle of your forehead (sometimes called the third eye), or to the top of your head.

Whenever your mind takes off in thought or your imagination soars in fantasy, you can use the HU chant or the breathing technique to bring yourself back to the present moment. As soon as you notice your mind wandering, gently direct your attention back to the object of your focus, the sound or the breath. You may have to repeat this process often. It is the mind's nature to wander, so be patient with yourself.

When you were a baby learning to walk, you didn't scold yourself when you fell down. You got up and tried again. Falling is just part of the process of learning to walk. This is the model of how we learn anything—including how to live. It's all about bringing ourselves back to the present, again and again. We love, then forget to be loving, then remember and become loving again. The more we remember to love, the more habitual loving will become. It's a matter of being present in every moment.

OBSERVATION

So often we read self-help books and make resolutions to change, then rush headlong into our daily lives, forgetting everything we learned. A Zen saying comes to mind: "How you handle anything is how you handle everything." If you really pay close attention to your life, you'll learn everything you need to know to be happier and more successful.

You cannot climb the ladder if you ignore some of the rungs. You have to climb and experience every single one of them. Those you avoid become your stopping places, your places of contraction.

You cannot go on until you have the courage to step on each rung and, by loving it, lift yourself up.

Observation is an important skill to practice. It allows you to stay present so that you can look at whatever is going on in your life with loving neutrality.

Let's take something everybody feels at times—impatience—and see how observation can change our experience of it. When we're impatient, we want what we want when we want it. Impatience distracts us from seeing the reality of a situation. We focus only on

> Keep in mind that this world is conditioned energy, and what you are reaching for is a loving that is unconditional.
>
> That loving is always available, but you must be available to it, without conditions.

how we'd like it to be. And trying to do something about our impatience usually makes us *more* impatient.

The solution is just to observe. Observe the situation, observe your feelings, observe your behavior. Observe whatever is happening neutrally, without internal comment, or judgment, or taking a position on it. You are observing only what is, not what you know or don't know about the situation. Look at the situation with fresh eyes. As you continue to observe, you will eventually reach a state of inner calm and contentment, and your impatience will disappear.

Observing is not doing nothing. Neutral observation is active and dynamic. The internal power that comes from practicing it is tremendous.

THE POWER OF ATTENTION

Cultivating a spiritual life can be a challenge, because our bodies, minds, and emotions—not to mention outside distractions— are constantly vying for our attention. It can be difficult to have a quiet life, never mind an inner life.

The idea that technology saves us time doesn't seem to be the reality. Nearly everyone I know has less time than ever before, and there are still only twenty-four hours in a day. Rather than saying we don't have enough time, it's more accurate to say we have too many options. As soon as we reduce our options, time opens up.

Still, everywhere we go, there are distractions. We've nearly all had the experience of being with someone in a bar or restaurant where there's a television set tuned to a sports game. You're talking to your friend, he's watching the game, and you're wondering why you're wasting your time.

There is never a good enough reason to take away your loving. You have the ability not to care for people's personalities and still love every human being for who they are. You can prefer not to be involved with someone acting negatively, and still love the person even if the action is not to your liking.

You can be in the most beautiful, romantic restaurant, eating a magnificent meal, but if your dinner partner isn't paying attention to you, the evening is likely to be a disaster. On the other hand, you can be in a cheap dive, eating mediocre food, but if your companion is giving you undivided attention, the evening will be fantastic.

Giving one another our full attention is so rare these days. At the first sign of quiet, our phones and pagers rush in. Invariably, just as you're about to say, "I love you," someone's cell phone rings.

When you're next in front of a mirror, look at yourself. Look yourself in the eye. If you don't like what you see, it's just another aspect of yourself for you to love.

If you start to feel the quality of loving drop away or go stagnant, it's time to stop and take another close look at what you are doing. Perhaps you forgot to love where you are. Truly, truly, truly, you must love everything you see.

The quality of attention is particularly important in approaching Spirit or God. When we sit down to meditate or pray, we want to bring our full attention to the moment. The challenge is that our minds, bodies, emotions, and imagination want our attention, too. They are constantly waving at us and shouting, "What about me?" Luckily, God doesn't care. He's not waving at us. He waits patiently for us to give Him our attention.

Sometimes, however, the distractions seem overwhelming. Maybe you sit down to meditate and then find the seat is not quite right. So you fidget a little until you're sitting comfortably. Then, you feel thirsty. You get up to get a glass of water before you settle down again. Then, you have to go to the bathroom. You go to the bathroom, come back and sit down, and the phone rings. You fret about whether or not to answer it, and decide to let the answering machine pick up. Then you wonder who was calling and get up to listen to the message, only to find out it was someone trying to sell you long-distance service. You sit down again and think about why you wasted time getting up. Finally, you settle in and sit quietly for a moment. Then the alarm goes off to remind you it's time to leave for work.

The best part of a spiritual approach to living is that it's all inside of us. Wherever we are, whatever we're doing, we can be leading an uplifting spiritual life. It's not about sitting on a meditation cushion (though that can be helpful when you set aside the time). It's not about being with the right group of people (though fellowship can be very supportive). It's not about the clothes you wear or the diet you eat. It's not about the shape of your body or where you live or work.

Regardless of behavior, appearance, or presentation, every human being is involved in their own particular rate of spiritual progress. Their own rate is their divine right. It's of much greater value to love them than to judge or criticize them.

It's not about what church, or mosque, or temple you belong to or how often you attend. You are the temple, the place of worship. All you need to do to realize that is to *pay attention.*

REFLECTIONS ON LOVING

Let each loving relationship you have
with another person live primarily inside you.
If you place it in the world,
you will experience difficulty.

There are no relationships "out there."
All of your relationships are inside you.
Outside is only the reflection
of what you are doing inside.

Ultimately, each relationship you have with another
person reflects your relationship with yourself.

Loving is a matter of giving of yourself
100 percent at any moment.
If you are married, give 100 percent
to the marriage and to your spouse.

If you hold back or place conditions on the marriage,
and keep part of your loving in reserve,
you will never know what that marriage could have been.
You will never know where the expression
of loving could have led you.

If you love 99 percent and do not go the full 100 percent,
you will end up in lack. There will be something lacking
and you will know it.

When you investigate and explore loving 100 percent,
there is no unknown area and thus no fear.

CHAPTER 5

VICTIM NO MORE

*We have a constant opportunity to love people past
their behavior, to love them unconditionally, and then
turn around and do the same thing towards ourselves.*

Playing the victim is one of the biggest games on the planet. When you allow your emotions and reactivity to dictate the way you approach life, you are very likely to feel like a victim.

You may believe strongly that your feelings are justified because of the pain and struggle you have endured. But your pain and struggle don't make you special. Everyone has pain and struggles in life. Ultimately, you are the one who makes yourself a victim. You victimize yourself by letting your emotions run your life.

In every difficult situation that you can't control, there is only one practical option: *Embrace it anyway*. In other words, make the choice to love, or accept wholeheartedly, whatever is happening. When you actively *choose* what is already happening, you take ownership of the situation and cease to be a victim of it. Even when all hell breaks loose, if you can say, "I love this and I love me, regardless," you will not feel as if you are at the mercy of life's ups and downs. You may need to say "I love this" more than once before you start to feel better, but once you start, you won't look back. (For more ways to work with this phrase, see **Practice 3:** **"I Love This,"** on page 25.)

Love yourself for being
"hard-headed."

Love yourself for not being
able to play a guitar and
sing and write music.

Love yourself for being a
"good-for-nothing."
You are such a lovely one.

Love yourself,
even when you don't
know what's going on.

Even when you don't feel
like loving, love the feeling
of not feeling loving.

Here's a story that shows how easy it is to allow ourselves to become victims:

When baby elephants are trained, the trainers take a large chain and wrap it around the elephant's leg and then fasten it to a big stake that is anchored deep in the ground. Then they let the baby elephant pull and pull until it realizes it can't go anywhere. They do this for two or three years, and then they take a small stake and pound it into the ground and tether the elephant to it with a rope. The elephant, having learned from its past experience, never even tries to move the stake. In that way, a huge animal becomes victim to a flimsy piece of rope and is as firmly held by that rope as if it were bound by iron chains. When we play the victim, we are behaving like this elephant. Yet all it takes is one fresh look, one totally new thought, to free us completely.

Animals don't have as many choices as humans do. But we *do* have choices, and we can choose to use everything that happens in our lives for our upliftment and growth. The story about the elephant is a wonderful one to help us see where we are allowing ourselves to be victimized by the past. What is your small stake? What event or experience of many years ago is holding you back now?

TAKING RESPONSIBILITY

A big part of letting go of being a victim is coming to a place where you can take complete responsibility for yourself and your relationships with others. That includes being responsible for your feelings, thoughts, and actions.

We are conditioned to look out in the world for the source of our fulfillment. And when things don't go the way we want, we try to find someone or something to blame. Attempting to control is a way of playing the Game of Life—the smaller game—trying to make life work. But, as I've mentioned, life *already* works. Placing the blame outside ourselves is a misguided attempt to regain a sense of control.

The fact is, we never were in control. We never had any control to lose. We don't have control over anything outside ourselves. Life is always happening according to its rules, not ours. When we move into full cooperation with life, it can appear that we're in control, but in reality, we are simply in a harmonious flow with life.

*There is no way
you can separate
yourself from love
and maintain freedom.
The only freedom
is to love it all.*

*You can be
everything you
want to be as soon
as you unconditionally
become unconditional.*

*Loving is the key.
Total, unconditional
loving.*

What we *are* in control of is what's inside us. We can't change someone else's mind, but we can change our own in an instant. We can't make someone love us, but we can always choose to be loving. Instead of attempting to control things outside ourselves, we can turn our attention to the bigger game, the Game of Love.

We can live without blaming others. We can allow them to express their own uniqueness. We don't need to insist that they change; insisting that others change is a form of fighting.

In truth, every one of our relationships resides inside us. Relationships are not "out there"; they are a reflection of what's going on in our own minds and hearts. The demands we project onto others are often demands we are making of ourselves. No wonder most of us are tense—we're carrying the weight of all our expectations, projected onto others.

To avoid playing the victim or blaming others, we need to keep our relationships up to date and present. That means making sure not to base our behavior on what happened last night or last week or last month—or twenty years ago. When you let go inside, you can be present here and now with the one relationship over which you *do* have control: your relationship with yourself.

FORGIVENESS

One way we undermine ourselves and stay stuck in the past is through the "story" we tell ourselves about our lives. Our individual story explains why we are the way we are, giving us the reasons we need to justify our behavior. The only problem is, for the most part, the story is fiction. There may be just enough truth to give it credibility—in our own minds, at least. But when we live our lives based on our

"But seek first the kingdom of God... and all these things shall be added to you."[3] Through misinterpretation of that statement, man has worshiped an outer God, looking for God somewhere in a church building, a temple, a tabernacle, on the top of a mountain, on the bottom of the ocean, on the moon, and so on.

We did not hear the rest of the directive, which is, "The kingdom of God is within you."[4] You can't be much more specific than that.

story, we are essentially living an illusion. In order to have an authentic life, we need to dismantle that illusion, to leave behind our story of restriction and contraction.

In the outer world, you can identify things rather objectively, and you can get a lot of people to go along with your identification. You can possess a definite object and place your joys and hopes on it. At some point, however, you may realize that fulfillment is not "out there." Fulfillment is within. Your happiness, your well-being, your love, and your success are all within you.

The heavenly things, the invisible things, are the spiritual things that are going to endure forever. Establish yourself in that area. It is within you.

What is the story you tell yourself about why you are not as successful as you'd like to be in your relationships, health, finances, or career? Does the story start at birth? In childhood? In more recent years? Is it related to lack—not enough love, money, or attention? Is the problem dysfunctional parents, or persecution because of your race, religious beliefs, or sexual orientation? (When in doubt, we can always blame our religion, our culture, or our beliefs to explain why we have closed down and contracted.)

As you think about your story, what consistent themes emerge? (Usually there is a point at which you began to feel like a victim.) What judgments did you make—and perhaps are still making—about yourself, about others, about the world, about God? In other words, what is negatively charged for you in those areas?

An important tool for clearing up the past and bringing your story up to date is forgiveness. More specifically, self-forgiveness. Forgiving ourselves is a difficult concept to grasp, because it goes against our conditioning.

To many people, forgiveness is absolution of some sort. A priest or other religious authority pardons you for your wrongdoing. Or you decide to let go of your negative feelings towards someone for hurting you in some way.

There is another way to look at forgiveness, one you may not have considered. In this approach, you don't forgive the *other person* for what you think they've done to you; rather, you forgive *yourself* for holding on to a *judgment* about what you think they did. And if *you're* the one who did something unloving to someone else, you use the same approach—forgiving yourself for holding on to a judgment about your behavior.

You can say "I forgive you" to someone you think has harmed you. You can apologize to someone *you* have hurt. But in reality, doing that is beside the point. *Everyone is already forgiven by God.* The person we've judged is already forgiven, and so, for that matter, are we. But if we're holding any negativity towards another, then we need to forgive *ourselves.* Even if the other person is long gone from our lives, we're still carrying them inside. So it is inside us that we need to make peace. In forgiving ourselves, the weight of the negative judgment is lifted.

Self-forgiveness is not an act of contrition or penance. It is a profound and radical approach to letting go of tensions and problems and preoccupations. When you hold a judgment against someone else, you are holding it inside your own body. It's much easier to let go and forgive yourself.

God is in the business of forgiveness. As I look at life on this planet, I often think that maybe *our* job as humans is to make sure God stays in business. (Then again, maybe God put us here to get the necessary training to go into *His* business.)

You may be wondering how self-forgiveness works. The practice below offers some suggestions.

PRACTICE 8

Forgiveness

Forgiveness is one of the fastest and most effective ways of releasing upsets, tensions, and judgments. All you need to do is forgive *yourself* for the judgments you have made.

Forgiving yourself for your judgments usually releases the negative charge you have on yourself or the situation. To begin the process, you can simply say, "I forgive myself for judging...," then add a reference to the person or issue in question. When you do this, you will often find that, almost miraculously, something lets go inside and you feel as if a weight has lifted.

Statements of forgiveness can be very general: "I forgive myself for judging my mother." However, if you do not experience a release of judgment, it might help to be more specific: "I forgive myself for judging my mother for not buying me the pair of shoes I wanted."

Perhaps you've hurt someone else—hurt their feelings, for example—but the other person isn't around, so you can't apologize directly. In that case, you might say, "I forgive myself for judging myself for anything I may have done to _____ *[fill in the person's name]* in _____ *[fill in a descriptive word or phrase]* situation."

How can you tell if you've released the judgment? You might spontaneously let out a sigh or take a deep breath. You might feel a surge of energy or warmth in your body, or a feeling of relief. Whenever you make a judgment against another person, it is stored in your body. Forgiving yourself releases the other person from your energy field.

As you go through your day, give yourself forgiveness breaks. Take ten seconds to sit quietly and forgive yourself for judging yourself or others.

If you observe yourself closely, you'll notice that the dark parts of you surface because they are looking for love. The best thing you can do is give them that love. As the poet Rainer Maria Rilke wrote, "Perhaps everything terrible is, in its deepest being, something helpless that wants help from us."

Forgiveness is an essential teaching of every major faith tradition. But it is more than a spiritual exercise. There is medical evidence that forgiveness is good for your health. An article on the ABC News web site reported the findings of a study indicating that when people forgive, their blood pressure drops.[5] Individuals who are the most unforgiving tend to have the highest blood pressure.

According to Carl Thoresen, director of the Stanford University Forgiveness Research Project, skeptics have ignored forgiveness research in the past. But, he suggests, these new findings open the door to accepting forgiveness as a viable way to manage conflict. "Forgiveness is not just a religious concept but is something that we can and should strive toward," Thoresen says. "[To forgive] is the most courageous act one can do."[6]

It takes extra courage to be forgiving when someone has done something especially hurtful. But forgiveness does not mean that you excuse or condone bad behavior. It is simply a way to lay down the burden of judgment and hurt you are carrying so that you can move on. As we saw earlier, when you're angry, you're the one who suffers. Thoresen sums it up when he says: "Resentment is the poison that you take yourself [while hoping] that the other person will die."

So, make peace with yourself and everyone around you. For example, you can forgive yourself for judging yourself for not doing the best you could. You can forgive yourself for judging yourself for judging. And you can forgive yourself for forgetting you are a loving, spiritual being.

As you forgive yourself and let go, you can say to yourself: "That's no longer real, it no longer exists, and my life begins anew from this moment on."

PERFECTLY PLACED FOR YOUR FUTURE SUCCESS

Many people see themselves as the sum of the past, the result of everything they've accumulated along the way. That's one way to look at life.

I prefer to look at it another way. As I see it, the person I am today is perfectly positioned for my future. The future, not the past, has conspired to put me where I am in this moment, in this place, in this position in my life, so that I can claim the potential that awaits me.

You, too, are perfectly placed for your future. From that perspective, you can tell yourself the story of your success. Your success is where love is leading you. Be specific as you describe your success in the area you wish to improve. Don't hold back. See, hear, feel your new attitude and new approach *as if you are already living it*. Think of this as your story of expansion.

Don't lose in your fantasy. Always win in your fantasy because you're making it up. Don't make it up bad, make it up good.

Be sure to make this a *success* fantasy. Give it a happy ending. It is a quirk of human nature that even when the possibilities are endless, as they are in fantasy, we tend to imagine ourselves losing. While making up your story, be happy—no, be *joyous*—as you contemplate the best outcome for yourself.

Perhaps by now you understand that you have made up a story about your past. Certain things happened, of course, but you probably embellished them, and then made up a philosophy to justify your decisions and actions. Now you can make up a new story, with a new philosophy, and begin to live it.

REFLECTIONS ON LOVING

Do you love someone because you love them,
or because of the way they love you?
Do you love someone because of their personality,
body, behavior, money, or position in the world?
Do you try to control the one you love
so that they behave the way you wish?

Control patterns we learn when we are very young
are often unconsciously expressed in our adult life.
If the child does not perform according to the adults' standards,
the adults often will withdraw their love so that the children
will do what is desirable in order to receive love.

How many times have you withdrawn your
expression of love because someone else didn't do
what you wanted, the way you wanted it?
Control over another cannot be exercised
if you stay within the consciousness of loving.

Even in the midst of conflict, you can allow love to lead you.
I have seen a husband and wife argue with each other
as if the conflict between them was catastrophic.
Then I would see the same couple the next day,
and they would be loving each other as if nothing happened.

Something did happen.
One of them listened to love's voice calling, then followed.

Most arguments between husbands and wives are about loving.
The yearning underneath the words is usually
the person asking to be loved as they are,
without demand for change, without judgment.

Listen for love.
Love knows that you got married for a good reason,
and that was to learn how to live and love unconditionally.

CHAPTER 6

THE BLESSINGS ALREADY ARE

*Although you may not know it yet, God's plan for you,
for your neighbor, and for the world, is perfect.*

The story of Jacques Lusseyran, a hero of the French Resistance in World War II, is an extraordinary example of how to find joy in difficult circumstances—and how *not* to feel like a victim, regardless of what happens.[7] Lusseyran had an idyllic childhood until age eight, when he was blinded in a schoolroom accident. He soon discovered that despite his total blindness, he could see an inner radiance. The catch was, he could only see the light when he was loving. When he was overcome with anger, impatience, competitiveness, or fear, the light immediately dimmed or went out altogether. In those moments, he said, he felt truly blind.

During World War II, after the Nazis occupied France, Lusseyran joined the resistance movement. He was captured and sent to the concentration camp at Buchenwald. Of the two thousand French interned there, Lusseyran was one of only thirty who survived. Later, he wrote that his experience in the camp confirmed two important truths: that each person's life is shaped from the inside, and that fear kills, but joy sustains life.

At Buchenwald, Lusseyran met a remarkable old man named Jeremy, who, despite the wretched conditions in the camp, radiated a joyful and healing presence. Jeremy managed not to judge the situation or his captors harshly. Lusseryan noticed that the prisoners who died the soonest were those who saw themselves as being in hell. In contrast, Jeremy never thought of himself as a victim or as one of the good guys against the bad. To Jeremy, life at Buchenwald was simply human beings carrying on as usual. Jeremy explained that before he came to Buchenwald, he had seen people living in fear and doing harm to themselves. It was the same in the camp; only the setting differed. Buchenwald is within each of us, Jeremy was saying. It is our minds that make it a hell and stoke its horrors. Therefore, we have the power within us to choose differently.

Somehow Jeremy had the inner resources to find joy in the midst of the horror. "He found it during moments of the day when others found only fear," Lusseyran recalled. Jeremy had managed to break the habit of judgment that makes us call adversity "evil" and feel victimized by it, Lusseyran concluded. "He had touched the very depth of himself and liberated...the essential, that which does not depend on any circumstance."

The psychiatrist Viktor Frankl, author of *Man's Search for Meaning*,[8] also spent time in concentration camps during World War II. From his experience at Auschwitz, he developed a therapeutic approach—logotherapy, from *logos*, the Greek word for "meaning"—that encourages us to look within our suffering for the deeper purpose of our lives. Frankl said that we should not waste our time questioning life, asking, "Why is this happening to me?" Instead, we should let life question *us*.

Here's how that might work in an everyday situation. Say you are caught in traffic. Instead of asking, "Why is there so much traffic?" you might consider a question that the traffic jam raises: "How patient can I be?" Seen from that perspective, even the most frustrating situation becomes an opportunity to observe and learn.

> The first commandment is to love God. The second is to love your neighbor.

A concentration camp is an extreme example of hardship. But the experiences of survivors like Lusseyran and Frankl teach us an important basic truth: we can't always chose our circumstances, but we *can* choose our attitude towards them. We continually have a choice about where to direct our attention—towards being a victim, or towards living in our loving essence.

Time and again, we hear of people who have gained strength from adversity and reached a place of loving despite unimaginable suffering. The challenge is to discover the gift, the joy, in each new situation as life reveals itself—to find, in fact, an opportunity for upliftment, learning, and growth.

ACCEPTANCE: THE FIRST LAW OF SPIRIT

Most human suffering arises in the gap between what we think *should be* and what *is*. It's here that we find our unresolved problems, worries, complaints, and judgments about the unfairness of life, as well as our fantasies about how we would like things to be.

We can always come up with good reasons for our behavior: we need the money, our families expect it, we owe it to society, and so on. Our stories and reasons and excuses are always "perfect"—and so are everybody else's. When someone does something you don't like, you can be sure they have a perfect explanation for it, just as you do for your own behavior.

Acceptance has been called the first "law" of Spirit—and for good reason. If you can accept *what is*, there is no conflict in life. There are no problems. There is no story. Accepting a situation, just as it is, closes the gap between *what should be* and *what is*.

The idea of acceptance often brings up a lot of *yes, buts*: "Yes, but if I accept things passively, the world will go down the tubes." You probably have your objections lined up already. But if you can allow yourself to really move into acceptance, even for a few seconds, you will find an immediate way out of the dilemmas created by your "shoulds."

Acceptance is not a passive state. Far from it. Acceptance is active because it requires you to be highly attentive. Acceptance has infinite subtleties and shadings. When you truly walk through the door of acceptance, you will experience joy and peace. You will be in the now. You will find yourself in your loving.

When we make a big effort towards results we want, we often get into a tension-producing situation. That can set up resistance, and resistance can create defensiveness. When we move into acceptance, we let go of tension and resistance, and allow results to come to us in a natural way.

Many people find acceptance just before they die. They let go. Nothing bothers them. They find peace, and love shines from their eyes. It's a blessing just to be in their presence.

Do we really have to wait until we're dying to discover the blessing in acceptance?

It seems easy to love God, until you realize that in loving God, you must love everything, including the neighbors. The neighbors may irritate and upset you, and that irritation closes the door to your own inner paradise.

When you love both your neighbor and your irritation, the doors open once again.

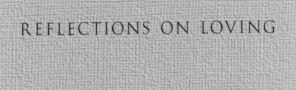

REFLECTIONS ON LOVING

When you choose to accept rather than demand change,
when you chose to support rather than criticize,
you choose to love rather than hurt, that is when
something inside you stands up and cheers.

Your heart may feel as if it could burst with
the fullness of loving. Then, instead of trying to control
a relationship, you will find that you can let go and
just be in relationship.

There's nothing for you to do but be natural,
and the most natural, God-like act is simply loving.

Have you ever found that the only good
thing about suffering is when it stops?

When the suffering stops,
you feel that you have learned something,
so you think that the suffering was good for you.
But you could have learned without the suffering.

How do you let go of those things in your
consciousness that no longer serve you?
The answer is to open up to greater love.
Love will go in and stir the pain
that you've locked away from even yourself.
As it is stirred, it will begin to surface and release.

You have the ability to raise yourself.
Don't contract from your experiences.
Bless them. Love them.
They are your ladders into expansion and higher consciousness.

You do not have to force your awakening or push the speed
of your unfoldment. You can, however, assist the process by
loving yourself every step of the way, and by
treating the people around you with kindness and honesty.

When you confront your challenges in life,
rise to the highest point within you, which is love.
There you will find the key to the Kingdom.

But there is a catch.
The love must encompass all things.
You must love your depression, love your despair,
love your anger, love your confusion, and love your upset.

If you bring irritation to people,
love the irritation and the people.
Sometimes you are a master of irritation.
Wouldn't you rather be a master of love?

CHAPTER 7

LET GO AND LET GOD

In order to expand into a higher level of consciousness, you must have less holding you here. You must let go.

Most of us are living out of one or more belief systems: our parents', our religion's, at the very least, our culture's. What we claim as our own beliefs are, most likely, beliefs we've inherited from others. Practical spirituality asks us to examine all our beliefs and put them to a simple test: *Is this belief working for me?* By that I mean, does it enhance your life in a positive way? Does it give you a sense of expansion?

You will know intuitively when a belief is not working for you because there will be contraction in your consciousness. Contraction often manifests as tension or upset, or even physical illness. Whenever you are experiencing contraction, try the following exercise:

Ask yourself: What is no longer working for me? *Just because something worked for you in the past doesn't mean it will continue to do so.*

Then, make a list of everything that isn't working for you.

Imagine letting go of one of those things.

What would you let go of? Could you let go of it now?

When you awaken each morning, it might be nice if you asked for the peace of God to be with you and all that you touch that day.

If you ask for attunement each day, it will change the quality of your life.

If you are one with God's consciousness, no man can come against you.

No matter what has happened in your life, you don't have to carry that experience around with you. It's important for your health and well-being to release the past, move into the present, and make this moment work for you.

LETTING GO OF CONTROL

Acknowledging what you are hanging on to is the essential first step to letting it go. Denial won't make something go away. In fact, the act of denying something actually affirms its existence, because you're putting energy into it. If, for example, you spilled something on the floor that you can't be bothered to clean up, every time you see the thing, your energy will go into stepping around it. Similarly, denying a loss or an upset or a disappointment requires you to invest a lot of mental energy in avoiding the subject.

You have to risk letting go of what no longer works for you in order to move into what does work. When you allow yourself to let go of negative thoughts and emotions, you create a space that can then be filled with your loving.

Perhaps you've heard the expression, "Let go and let God." *Letting go* is a way of saying to yourself, "Relax. You're not in charge." *Letting God* is a way of saying, "Be patient. Everything will be taken care of."

God is already present inside you. You just need to be patient as that truth reveals itself to you. As you relax and listen within, you will automatically start to attune yourself to the presence of God. With that awareness, you can begin to let God take charge. As you "let God" handle your life, problems in the outside world will have less power over you, and you will experience more love and forgiveness for yourself and others. Letting go and letting God leads to inner freedom.

Let go of pain and guilt, and they will no longer be driving you.

PRACTICE 9

Letting Go and Letting God

Letting go and letting God is another way of saying, "Relax, and be patient." Begin by bringing your attention to your breathing. As your breath flows into your belly, let go. Relax your shoulders, align your body with the flow of gravity, and release any tension down through your feet into the earth. Allow your head to "float" on top of your shoulders.

As you relax your body and focus on your breathing, it's remarkable how quickly you will come to a peaceful place within. This is the first step in connecting with your spirit, in attuning yourself to the presence of God.

You can sense the presence of Spirit by a shift in the quality of the energy around you. When you are in attunement, things just naturally feel better both within and around you.

Whenever you want to call on God, all you need to do is sit quietly and listen. If nothing happens, and all you experience is stillness, that's wonderful, too. God is in that stillness.

FOR THE HIGHEST GOOD

Prayer has so many religious overtones that our preconceptions may prevent us from seeing how simple and effective it can be. Quite simply, prayer works. It doesn't have to be complicated, and it doesn't have to be ritualistic. A prayer can be just three or four words. Some people have remarkable success with simple prayers. An example of a simple prayer is "God help my health." Repeated at least once a day for a month, it can bring surprising results.

There is a growing body of scientific research confirming the power of prayer. In many cases, positive results are not associated with any particular religious tradition. One example is a now-famous study involving close to four hundred heart patients at San Francisco General Hospital.[9] Half the patients were given the latest high-tech medical treatment, while the other half, in addition to medical treatment, received prayers. Neither the patients nor the medical staff treating them knew which patients were being prayed for.

The results were remarkable. At just about every level, the patients who were prayed for did better than those who received medical treatment alone.

The loving nature will attract those things of a loving nature.

The Light in you will attract the Light in others.

Don't be afraid to take someone's hand.

Don't be afraid to hug people.

Share the love. Give it out.

The love will be greater in you as a result.

The group that received prayers had faster recovery and fewer deaths, and even those who died during the course of the study reported better quality of life and greater happiness in the days up to death than the heart patients who were not prayed for.

You might assume that the more specific a prayer is, the better it is. But research has shown that although specific, detailed prayer can produce results, what is even more effective is non-specific, general prayer.

A general prayer can be something like "Thy will be done." In other words, you put the results in God's hands, trusting that the outcome will be what is best for all concerned. Research shows that non-specific prayer is two to three times as effective as specific prayer. However much we think we know about what we need, it turns out that God really does know best.

At the end of every prayer, I add the phrase, "for the highest good of all concerned." Sometimes I shorten it to "for the highest good." In saying those words, I am acknowledging that I don't know what is best but that a higher intelligence does. I've even heard people say "this or better, for the highest good," to acknowledge that God may have far greater plans for us (or for others) than we, with our limited, human minds, can imagine.

Turning the outcome of our prayers over to God prevents our egos from interfering and helps us steer clear of trying to manipulate circumstances to our advantage at the expense of others.

PRACTICE 10

Prayer

What is your prayer, right now?

Keep it simple. Prayer does not have to be complicated.

Remember, you don't have to spell out all the details. All you need to do is place the situation in God's hands and let God handle the results. At the end of your prayer, you can add the phrase "for the highest good of all concerned," or just "for the highest good," to acknowledge that you might not know what's best in the situation but a higher power does.

Try repeating your prayer at least once a day, for the next month. See how it works for you. Saying a short prayer each day may sound ridiculously easy, but you would be surprised how much discipline it takes. Prayer practice involves not just the words you say but making good on your commitment to say them every day, without fail.

THE LIGHT

There's a tendency to think that if we worry enough about a situation, we can change it. I've found, however, that worry is not very effective in changing anything. In fact, it can increase tension in your body, mind, and emotions, which can make you feel worse. If you worry too much, you can become ill. And if you get ill, other people have to take care of you. So, by worrying, you may create more problems than you're trying to solve.

To find the peace within, it's often necessary to become quiet verbally so that you can hear the voice of love from within.

It's much easier to give your problems to God, or to the Light. You can take a problem or situation and say, "I place this in the Light for the highest good." It's amazing how freeing that is.

When I refer to "the Light," I mean the very highest and purest Light that exists. This Light is a spiritual force, an emanation of God that can be used as a practical tool for day-to-day living. The Light is present everywhere and in everyone. It is always available to you. But in order to gain assistance from the Light, you have to ask for it. Since this Light is everywhere at all times, when you "ask" for it, what you are really doing is asking *yourself* to be present with the Light. You are bringing your awareness to the Light. In that respect, working with the Light is similar to breathing practice. You are always breathing, but *consciously* bringing your awareness to your breath can be transformational. So it is with the Light.

As you attune to the Light, if you repeat silently, "I ask for the Light for the highest good," this will provide a form of support or protection for you. If you have situations or people you are concerned about, you can place them in the Light, and then let go, confident that the Light is with them. As you release problems into the Light, you may actually feel them lift from you, leaving you freer inside.

You can work with the Light anytime (see **Asking for the Light,** below). But just as in the practice of prayer, when you are using the Light, it is always best that your intention be for the highest good.

PRACTICE 11

Asking for the Light

Asking for the Light is a very effective and practical tool for letting go of your worries and concerns. It is a way of becoming present with the spiritual force of God. Here is a Light prayer that you can say at the beginning of the day, or whenever you feel you need more clarity or assistance in your life.

Start by sitting quietly and spending a few seconds relaxing with your breathing. Allow your mind and body to come to rest. Now, silently repeat the following words (or your own variation on them):

Dear God, I ask just now for the Light of God, the highest, purest Light, to be with me now, to surround me, to fill me, to fill this room or this space for the highest good. I ask that the Light go ahead of me this day so that I may grow inside and let go of anything that is no longer working for me. I ask that my heart be opened to loving. I ask that the Light be sent to my loved ones for the highest good.

If there are individuals you wish to place in the Light, you can silently say their names. If you are struggling with a particular problem, you can place that situation in the Light. Once you have placed a problem or concern in the Light, you can let it go, knowing that the Light is with it and that it is out of your hands. (If the situation later comes back to distract you, you can again place it in the Light.)

When you have finished placing people and situations in the Light, you can end your prayer with the following words: *I ask all of this in love, and I give my thanks.*

Sending the Light for the highest good to a person or situation—even a country—can be of great service. If you're concerned with the problems in the Middle East, for example, instead of lamenting how terrible the situation is, you can do something practical by sending the Light: "For the highest good, I ask for the Light to be sent to the Middle East." In effect, sending the Light is simply making a choice to use your own divine nature to assist.

How, you may ask, do we know if sending the Light helps or not? The only answer is practical experience. As we saw, prayer can work even when the person prayed for is unaware of it. In a situation as complex as the conflict in the Middle East, it might be difficult to see results directly, but that does not mean that nothing is happening. As you use the Light more and more in your life, you will begin to notice changes, and you will have your own experience to draw on.

REFLECTIONS ON LOVING

Don't resist the negativity within you. Love it.
Loving will purify and lift all negativity.

If you have a negative thought,
love the idea of having a negative thought.
That is the way to turn a stumbling block
into a stepping-stone.

Or, you can say,
"I don't have to travel that path," and then you don't.
Instead, you can let love lead you in another direction.

You have the right to direction.
In fact, once you let love lead,
it is your duty. If you don't perform this duty,
then the consequences lead you.
Consequences are your reaction instead of your action.

Love your consequences.
They are your opportunity to learn.
They are your opportunity to gain wisdom.
They are your opportunity to properly identify with what is true.

When you close yourself off, you can become depressed
because you miss the loving you once experienced.
If you cannot get in touch with and share the loving that
is present for you, then share your depression and anxiety.
Treat your loving and your depression as equal.

Anxiety, love, depression, and happiness
must all be treated equally. When you do,
there can be no place for anything "better" or "worse"
inside of you, so judgment ceases to have
power in your consciousness.

When you treat your depression the same as your loving,
then neither has more power than the other does
and you are free to choose the expression you want.

CHAPTER 8

A SPIRITUAL PERSPECTIVE

The One you have been waiting for is already here—and has been here for a long time. You are the spiritual being you've been searching to find.

As the Jesuit scientist and mystic Teilhard de Chardin once said, we are not human beings having a spiritual experience; we are spiritual beings having a human experience. That observation is a powerful reminder that how we define ourselves shapes how we experience life. It often seems to be easier for people to see themselves as villains than as heroes. But let's assume, for the moment, that you *are* a divine being, a spiritual being having a human experience. And let's assume you have divine powers. Take that a little further and assume that you are a *superhero* with *superpowers*.

What are your superpowers? You may be tempted to say, "What superpowers? I can't even get the laundry done on time." But remember, you're a divine being, and certain powers are your divine heritage. One of those powers is choice. That's an awesome power right there. So are some of the other ones: the power to love, for example, and the power to forgive.

Think about how you deny your superpowers. By comparing yourself to others, maybe, or dwelling on a perceived lack of self-worth, or overidentifying with outer symbols like social status, possessions, and money. To many people, superpower means the

Through loving, you can expand past the resistances and limitations of your life. You have the opportunity to change the flow of your life through your ability to be loving.

ability to control others. That's not a superpower; it's simply a desire for control. Real superpowers—such as the ability to change our life with a shift in perspective—come from within.

The question you may be asking about now is: *Why, if I have all these superpowers, am I not demonstrating them in my life?*

Do you remember the story of Superman? He was sent to Earth as a boy from the planet Krypton just before it exploded. On Earth, he has superpowers, and is invincible. Well, almost invincible. His one weakness is kryptonite—the substance his home planet was made of. When Superman is around kryptonite, he goes weak and his superpowers disappear. If he's around it long enough, he becomes so weak he could die.

What is your kryptonite? Your area of vulnerability? What causes you to go weak and lose your superpowers?

The most common ways we lose our superpowers are through judgments and feelings of being a victim. You may recall from the story about Jeremy that people in the concentration camp who saw themselves as victims died soonest. They let their belief rob them of their divine powers, including choice.

Maybe you're holding onto a judgment about what you did or didn't do. Perhaps you resent the way you were brought up, or your lack of education, or the person you chose to marry. You may indeed have an irrefutable story for why certain aspects of life have turned out as they have—and why you are justified in feeling like a victim as a result. But can you see how those feelings of judgment and victimhood are robbing you of your divine powers—your ability to choose a life of expansion, based on loving and forgiving, rather than a life of contraction, based on negativity and fear?

Instead of looking at your life and thinking you are restricted, move into the loving, knowing you can expand past any limitation and live in the freedom that is always with you.

Don't be willing to give over your superpowers so easily. Take a breath and take a moment to accept your superhero identity, which is a doorway to accepting yourself as a divine being. **Practice 12: Claiming Your Superpowers**, on the next page, can help you step into your superhero identity and reclaim your powers.

PRACTICE 12

Claiming Your Superpowers

Superman has his cape. Wonder Woman has her cuffs. Now that you've accepted your superhero identity—the divine nature at your core—what outward signs or symbols will help you remember the superpowers you possess?

First you need a name. A good place to start is with the quality you've chosen to develop (see **Getting Your Life Going,** pages 9 and 10). Are you Freddy the Forgiver? Paula the Peacemaker? Captain Compassion? Linda Loving?

Perhaps you'd also like a talisman? A magic wand? A cape? A special stone, or piece of jewelry? And what about a symbol, an image, a crest, or a banner?

Finally, you'll need a posture or gesture—your superhero stance. Observe how you hold your body, how you stand, how you move when you fully embrace your superhero identity and superpowers. What gestures do you make? What is your facial expression?

Whenever you experience difficulties or challenges in your life, or whenever you're in super-villain mode—angry, judgmental, resentful, playing the victim—if you assume your superhero posture, your attitude will very likely change to a positive one.

Many of us shut down—give away our power—when we encounter pain and suffering. We shrink from disturbing scenes, averting our eyes or avoiding them altogether. But when we let love lead us, we can access the superhero within us and meet those same disturbances without moving from our center. Life continually gives us opportunities to be fully present in our superhero capacity. We don't have to give up our power, our center.

A LOVING PERSPECTIVE

Over time, our beliefs and conditioning can build up and become more complex. They start to take on a life of their own. People may find themselves disagreeing about religious issues automatically, without even considering whether their responses are rational. It's easy to forget that the basis of most of the world's spiritual teachings is love. When people tell me they don't believe in God, I ask them if they have ever experienced love. Nearly always

Laughter is love being demonstrated, love being expressed. It's so good and healing to be able to laugh at yourself and with yourself.

If you take yourself too seriously, you are going to fall to your knees before too long and have the world on your back. That may be a very hard burden.

they say yes. To me, if you have experienced love, you have experienced God.

The New Testament says: "God is love, and he that dwelleth in love, dwelleth in God, and God in him."[10] If you think you don't know who God is, just ask yourself if you know love. If you do, then you know God.

When Jesus taught to love God with your body, mind, and soul, and love your neighbor as yourself,[11] he was drawing upon the Jewish religious tradition. These ideas did not originate with him. He was quoting from what we now refer to as the Old Testament.[12] Jesus added, "A new command I give you. Love one another. As I have loved you, so you must love one another.[13]

You may have noticed a common theme in the last paragraph: *Love* God with your body, mind, and Soul. *Love* your neighbor as yourself. *Love* one another as I have *loved* you. These words, to me, are the essential teachings of Jesus and of the Bible.

Looking at life from a spiritual perspective is a fascinating and engaging journey. You don't have to be in a big hurry to find God.

Rushing doesn't get you there any faster. God is present. We can all be present in our love, right now.

In recent years, a number of my friends have been dealing with cancer and several have died. What I inevitably hear from people who get cancer is: "That's it! I'm not going to push myself so much. I'm going to stop thinking negatively, and I'm going to relax more."

I have heard this theme repeated again and again, in various ways. Why do we have to wait to get cancer to change how we live? Instead, maybe we can just say to ourselves, "I'm not going to rush about and create stress. I'm going to be happy. I'm going to relax. And I am going to love because I want to, because it feels better, because it's healthier and more productive."

When you fight to maintain separation from other people, you will lock yourself into a position of pain.

Studies have shown that humor and laughter are good for the immune system.[14] So, even if you don't give time to the practices in this book, perhaps you've gleaned something from the medical research. Prayer is good for you. Forgiveness is good for you. Laughter is good for you. Breathing consciously is good for you. If you get nothing else from this book, maybe you'll understand these four simple truths.

REFLECTIONS ON LOVING

You're going to be another day older whether you do anything today or not. So this day, why not just say,

"I love you whether or not you love me."

That's the beginning of self-mastery. You'll have the freedom inside of you to say, "I love you when you're here. I love you when you're not here. If I never see you again, I'll still love you. If you go, I'll miss you, but that's the part of me that's conditioned to miss.
I'll get over it because I'm going to go on loving."

Sometimes you feel like you can't go on, but you do.
Look at all the times you've said
"I'll never live through this,"
and here you are, living through it.

When someone is angry or is fighting with you,
often the easiest demonstration of your love is silence.
That's one way to win, but it only works
if you truly maintain your center of love.

You give that love in a pure way, continuously,
like the pulling of a golden silk thread.
It's the best way to win,
because the other person gets to win, too.

Maintain your loving just a little while longer
than you think you need to.
Then you are becoming master of yourself.

When you try to master someone else, you haven't mastered
yourself. You become a taker. Then you are out of your
center of love, for loving is a giving action.

When you have mastered yourself,
you do not have to go any further.
You don't have to master anybody else
to prove you've mastered yourself.

CHAPTER 9

KEEPING UP THE MOMENTUM

Listen to the heart.
It will tell you truly wherein you live.

By now, I hope, the principle of letting love lead is alive inside of you. Whenever you become aware of a worry, a disturbance, or an imbalance, instead of contracting you can just observe it and say to yourself, "Oh, good, things are moving. Now, how can love lead me?" That thought will bring you back to yourself and reconnect you to your loving.

If that thought alone doesn't work, you can choose one of the practices you've learned in this book, and enter loving through another door. And if you find yourself resisting every suggestion, you can simply say to yourself, "I love myself for resisting everything"—and enter loving anyway.

It is a human tendency to look outside ourselves for recognition and approval. But as you've seen, when you do that, you are living from the outside in. In the long run you'll be dissatisfied. Letting love lead is living from the inside out. That's the way to true fulfillment.

WHERE ARE YOU NOW?

At the beginning of the book, you were asked to identify the area of your life in which you were experiencing the most movement. Movement, as I mentioned, often shows up as discomfort or dissatisfaction. But wherever there is movement, there is the greatest opportunity for change—and the momentum to let love lead.

Using the same scale of 0 to 10 (0 indicates no satisfaction or fulfillment; 10 indicates complete satisfaction), take a moment to calibrate what you are experiencing in this area now. Enter your answer below.

Relationships: _____   Finances: _____

Health: _____   Career: _____

How are you doing? How does your score compare with where you were when you started reading this book?

The final question: *Where does love lead you now?*

REFLECTIONS ON LOVING

When you can release the concept of
"I'm here and they're there," one day you will find
that you are in everybody's heart.
You won't perceive others as being less or more than you are.
You will know their heartaches and their joys
because they are, in essence, the same as yours.

Then you'll be so involved in finding
"you" in everybody around you that there just won't
be any room for boredom, anxiety, or depression.
You'll find the spiritual form that is "you"
in everything and everybody.
You'll find incredible beauty in everything.

If the heart sings a song of love, go.
If there is no response or there is doubt, steer clear.

This is your guide.

This is love leading you.

Notes

1 Ronald Kotulak, "Waking Up to the High Cost of Lost Sleep," *The Chicago Tribune,* Chicagoland Final Edition, News, May 31, 1998, p.1.

2 Carol Krucoff, "Stress and the Art of Breathing; Relaxation: Modern Medicine is Giving Nontraditional Breathing Principles a Closer Look," *Los Angeles Times,* Home Edition, July 10, 2000, p.1.

3 Matthew 6:33, New King James Version.

4 Luke 17:21, NIV.

5 Sara Adler, "Forgiveness May be Good For Your Health," abcnews.com, April 7, 2002, <http://abcnews.go.com/sections/living/DailyNews/forgiveness000407.html>

6 Sara Adler, "Forgiveness May be Good For Your Health," abcnews.com, April 7, 2002, <http://abcnews.go.com/sections/living/DailyNews/forgiveness000407.html>. Also, see: Stanford Forgiveness Program, <http://www.stanford.edu/~alexsox/forgiveness_article.htm>.

7 Jacques Lusseyran, *Against the Pollution of the I: Selected Writings of Jacques Lusseyran,* (Parabola Books 2000).

8 Viktor E. Frankl, *Man's Search for Meaning,* (Washington Square Press 1997).

9 R. Byrd, "Positive therapeutic effects of intercessory prayer in a coronary care unit population," Southern Med J. 81:826-829 (1988).

10 1 John 4:16, King James Version.

11 Matthew 22:37, New International Version.

12 See: Deuteronomy 6:5, 11:13, and 13:3; Joshua 22:5.

13 John 13:34, New International Version.

14 Steven M. Sultanoff, Ph.D., "Survival of the Witty-est: Creating Resilience through Humor," *Therapeutic Humor,* Publication of the American Association for Therapeutic Humor Vol. XI, 5, p. 1-2 (Fall 1997), <http://www.humormatters.com/articles/resilience.htm>.

POSTSCRIPT

We hope this introduction to practical spirituality has been helpful. We welcome your comments on *Momentum: Letting Love Lead* and on your experiences in doing the Practices. You may send us an email at momentum@mandevillepress.org, or write or call us at:

Mandeville Press
P.O. Box 513935
Los Angeles, CA 90051-1935
323-737-4055
www.mandevillepress.org

If you would like to have a Momentum workshop in your area, send in the card enclosed in this book or contact us at the above address.

If you've enjoyed this book, you may want to explore and delve more deeply into what John-Roger has shared about this and other related topics. For more information on John-Roger's teachings through the Movement of Spiritual Inner Awareness, contact:

MSIA®
P.O. Box 513935
Los Angeles, CA 90051
800-899-2665
soul@msia.org
www.msia.org

ADDITIONAL RESOURCES
AND STUDY MATERIALS

The following materials can support you in learning more about the ideas presented in *Momentum: Letting Love Lead*.

BOOKS BY JOHN-ROGER

SPIRITUAL WARRIOR: THE ART OF SPIRITUAL LIVING

Full of wisdom, humor, common sense, and hands-on tools for spiritual living, this book offers practical tips to take charge of our lives and create greater health, happiness, abundance, and loving. Becoming a spiritual warrior has nothing to do with violence. It is about using the positive qualities of the spiritual warrior—intention, ruthlessness, and impeccability—to counter negative personal habits and destructive relationships, especially when you are confronted with great adversity.

Hardbound book #0-14829-36-X, $20

RELATIONSHIPS: LOVE, MARRIAGE AND SPIRIT

This book offers practical and workable keys for improving our relationships. Pointing out that the ultimate relationship is the one you have with yourself, it provides guidance on how to relate more effectively with your spouse, children, significant other, boss, and co-workers, as well as information on sexual fulfillment, abortion, spiritual law, etc.

Included in the book are chapters on:
Relationship and Spiritual Law
The Subtle Traps of Communication
Sexual Fulfillment
Pain, the Awakener
The Price of Approval
Ending a Relationship
Hardbound Book #1-893020-05-3, $20

FORGIVENESS: THE KEY TO THE KINGDOM
Forgiveness is the key factor in personal liberation and spiritual progression. This book presents profound insights into forgiveness and the resulting personal joy and freedom. God's business is forgiving. This book provides encouragement and techniques for making it our business as well.
Softbound Book #0-914829-62-9, $12.95

INNER WORLDS OF MEDITATION
In this self-help guide to meditation, meditation practices are transformed into valuable and practical resources for exploring the spiritual realms and dealing with life more effectively. Included are a variety of meditations that can be used for gaining spiritual awareness, achieving greater relaxation, balancing the emotions, and increasing energy.
Softbound Book #0-914829-45-9, $12
6-Audiotape Packet #3915, $45
3-CD Set #3915-CD, $45

LOVING EACH DAY FOR PEACEMAKERS,
Choosing Peace Everyday

Peace? It's a noble idea, yet a seemingly elusive reality. Peace between nations is built upon peace between individuals, and peace between individuals depends upon peace within each person. Making peace more than just a theory or idea, *Loving Each Day for Peacemakers* guides readers to their own solutions for experiencing peace.

Hardbound book #1-893020-14-2, $12

PSYCHIC PROTECTION

In this book, John-Roger describes some of the invisible levels: the power of thoughts, the unconscious, elemental energies, and magic. More importantly, he discusses how to protect yourself against negativity that can be part of those levels. As you practice the simple techniques in this book, you can create a greater sense of well-being in and around you.

Softbound Book #0-914829-69-6, $6.95

RESOURCE MATERIALS BY JOHN-ROGER

The following resource materials are available through the Movement of Spiritual Inner Awareness, 800-899-2665, www.msia.org, order@msia.org.

TURNING POINTS TO PERSONAL LIBERATION

John-Roger presents direct, insightful information outlining the causes and cures of hurt, anger, confusion, jealousy, feelings of separation and loneliness, and other limiting behaviors and beliefs that often block our happiness, success and enjoyment.

These tapes contain practical keys and wisdom for gaining greater acceptance, understanding, loving, freedom, and liberation:

Keys to Handling Negative Emotions
Turning Hurt and Anger to Acceptance and Loving
5 Characteristics and Cures of Emotional Mood Swings
Ten of life's essential questions
Insecurity and what to do about it
Healing the Hurt

6-Audiotape packet #3916, $45

HEALTH FROM THE INSIDE OUT

This packet of three audiotapes outlines how to use the energy of the body to create better health. Included are insights into the cycle of overeating and practical methods for overcoming it. There is a description of how to use the power of thought for better health, as well as to connect with the Supreme Source to promote greater healing and vitality. These tapes also describe how we sometimes promote "dis-ease" and how to change those patterns to gain better physical balance.

Topics on the tapes include:

Adapting toward health or adopting dis-ease

Are you stuffing your expression?

Are you unconsciously depleting your energy?

Awakening beyond body consciousness

Body balance meditation

3-Audiotape packet #3909, $24.95

SUCCESS FROM THE INSIDE OUT

If you work hard, pay taxes, live "right," and still don't have what you want, this tape packet may be just the thing for you. Within the information it provides is a useful blueprint for discovering your innate abundance and your ability to create the life you dream of and deserve.

In this packet:

Discover the 8 essential steps to success

Learn the magic of attitude and gratitude

Awaken to greater opportunity and creativity

Utilize your inner power of focus, thoughts & words

Experience a meditation for creating wealth

4-Audiotape packet #3913, $24.95

OBSERVATION: THE KEY TO LETTING GO

In order to accept what is, we need to observe, like a scientist. "Observation," John-Roger says, "is the key to letting go and letting God." In observation, we are not getting involved with our

emotions or bringing preconceived assumptions to the situation. Learning how to practice these principles more effectively can have tangible and profound benefits for bringing greater balance and happiness into our lives.
Audiotape #1552, $10

ARE YOU AVAILABLE TO YOURSELF?

Health, wealth, happiness, abundance, and riches are our heritage in this life. John-Roger reminds us that everything is available to us if we are available to ourselves and the spiritual life-force within us all.
Audiotape #7238, $10
Videotape #VC-7238, $20

SOUL AWARENESS DISCOURSES—A Course in Soul Transcendence

Soul Awareness Discourses are designed to teach Soul Transcendence, which is becoming aware of yourself as a Soul and as one with God, not as a theory, but as a living reality. They are for people who want a consistent, time-proven approach to their spiritual unfoldment.

A set of Soul Awareness Discourses consists of 12 booklets, one to study and contemplate each month of the year. As you read each Discourse, you can activate an awareness of your Divine essence and deepen your relationship with God.

Spiritual in essence, Discourses are compatible with religious beliefs you might hold. In fact, most people find that Discourses support the experience of whatever path, philosophy, or religion (if any) they choose to follow. Simply put, Discourses are about eternal truths and the wisdom of the heart.

The first year of Discourses addresses topics ranging from creating success in the world to working hand-in-hand with Spirit.

A yearly set of Discourses is regularly $100. MSIA is offering the first year of Discourses at an introductory price of $50. Discourses come with a full, no-questions-asked, money-back guarantee. If at any time you decide this course of study is not right for you, simply return it, and you will promptly receive a full refund.

To order Discourses, email order@msia.org or call 1-800-899-2665.

About the Authors

JOHN-ROGER

A teacher and lecturer of international stature, John-Roger is an inspiration in the lives of many people around the world. For over three decades, his wisdom, humor, common sense and love have helped people to discover the Spirit within themselves and find health, peace, and prosperity.

With two co-authored books on the *New York Times* Bestseller list to his credit, and more than three dozen spiritual and self-help books and audio albums, John-Roger offers extraordinary insights on a wide range of topics. He is the founder of the Church of the Movement of Spiritual Inner Awareness (MSIA), which focuses on Soul Transcendence; founder and Chancellor of the University of Santa Monica; President of Peace Theological Seminary & College of Philosophy; founder of Insight Transformational Seminars; and founder and President of The Institute for Individual and World Peace.

John-Roger has given over 5,000 lectures and seminars worldwide, many of which are televised nationally on his cable program, "That Which Is," through the Network of Wisdoms. He has been a featured guest on "Larry King Live," "Politically Incorrect," "The Roseanne Show," and appears regularly on radio and television.

An educator and minister by profession, John-Roger continues to transform lives by educating people in the wisdom of the spiritual heart.

For more information about John-Roger, you may also visit: www.john-roger.org

PAUL KAYE

Paul Kaye has been a dedicated student of spiritual thought and practices since his youth in England. His explorations have taken him into Yoga, Zen, and the spiritual foundations of movement and the martial arts.

Paul's interests include the philosophies of such poets and teachers as Lao Tzu, Rumi and Kabir and the esoteric teachings of Jesus Christ. Paul has designed workshops on the practical application of spiritual principles and presented them worldwide. Paul is a unique and remarkable presence. He brings an abundance of lightheartedness into whatever he does, and his presentations are inspiring, practical, and filled with a wonderful sense of humor and wisdom.

For over 30 years he has studied with renowned educator and author John-Roger and he is president of the Church of the Movement of Spiritual Inner Awareness (MSIA), an ecumenical, non-denominational church. Paul is an ordained minister and has a doctorate in spiritual science.

For author interviews and speaking engagements, please contact Angel Gibson at:

Mandeville Press
3500 West Adams Blvd.
Los Angeles, CA 90018
323-737-4055 x 155
angel@mandevillepress.org

We welcome your comments and questions.

Mandeville Press
3500 West Adams Blvd.
Los Angeles, Ca. 90018
323-737-4055
www.mandevillepress.org
jrbooks@mandevillepress.org